T0400815

Visit and Learn

The Statue of Liberty

by Diana Murrell

www.focusreaders.com

Focus Readers is distributed by North Star Editions:
sales@northstareditions.com | 888-417-0195

Produced for Focus Readers by Red Line Editorial.

Photographs ©: Shutterstock Images, cover, 1, 4, 7, 13, 16, 21, 22, 25, 26, 29; Nadar/Heritage Art/ Heritage Images AiWire/Newscom, 8; Hum Images/Alamy, 11; iStockphoto, 14–15, 19

Library of Congress Cataloging-in-Publication Data
Names: Murrell, Diana, author.
Title: The Statue of Liberty / by Diana Murrell.
Description: Lake Elmo, MN : Focus Readers, [2024] | Series: Visit and
 learn | Includes index. | Audience: Grades 2-3
Identifiers: LCCN 2023000097 (print) | LCCN 2023000098 (ebook) | ISBN
 9781637396209 (hardcover) | ISBN 9781637396773 (paperback) | ISBN
 9781637397879 (pdf) | ISBN 9781637397343 (ebook)
Subjects: LCSH: Statue of Liberty (New York, N.Y.)--Juvenile literature.
Classification: LCC F128.64.L6 M88 2024 (print) | LCC F128.64.L6 (ebook)
 | DDC 974.7/1--dc23/eng/20230104
LC record available at https://lccn.loc.gov/2023000097
LC ebook record available at https://lccn.loc.gov/2023000098

Printed in the United States of America
Mankato, MN
082023

About the Author

Diana Murrell is a writer and teacher. She enjoys visiting famous monuments in the United States. When she is not writing, Diana likes to bake and explore nature trails.

Table of Contents

Chapter 1

Lady Liberty

In 1886, France gave the United States a birthday present. It was a huge statue. The statue stands 305 feet (93 m) tall. It became known as the Statue of Liberty.

 **The official name of the statue is *Liberty Enlightening the World.***

The statue shows a woman standing on broken chains. Her crown has seven rays of light. She wears a long robe. In her right hand, she holds a torch. In her left hand, she holds a tablet.

The Statue of Liberty is a famous **monument**. It stands on Liberty

Did You Know?

The outside of the statue is made of copper. This metal is reddish-brown. But over time, sunlight and rain turn it green.

 New York Harbor lies between the states of New Jersey and New York.

Island in New York City. This island is in New York Harbor. Millions of people visit the statue every year.

Chapter 2

Planning and Building

French writer Édouard de Laboulaye loved the United States. In 1865, he had an idea. He wanted to give the United States a gift. The country had been **independent** for nearly 100 years.

Édouard de Laboulaye often wrote about freedom and ending slavery.

Laboulaye needed help. So, he talked to Frédéric-Auguste Bartholdi. Bartholdi was a French artist. He designed a statue. He used several **symbols**. The crown and torch are symbols of hope. The tablet and broken chains are symbols of freedom.

Bartholdi wanted the statue to be huge. That meant it had to be strong. So, he talked to Gustave Eiffel. Eiffel was a French **engineer**. He made sure the statue would be

stable. Richard Morris Hunt was an

American **architect**. He designed a

pedestal for the statue.

Many French workers helped build the statue. They spent nine years building it. Then they carefully took the statue apart. They packed the 350 pieces into many boxes. A ship carried the boxes to New York City.

The pedestal took two years to build. After that, workers rebuilt

Did You Know?

People in the United States gave $100,000 for the pedestal. That would be worth $3 million today.

the statue on top of it. In October 1886, the Statue of Liberty was finally complete.

Three Layers

The Statue of Liberty has three layers. The inner layer is a metal tower. It has many braces. They are shaped like triangles. This shape is very strong.

The next layer is a frame. It goes around the metal tower. The frame can sway. It moves up to 3 inches (8 cm) in the wind. That keeps the statue from breaking.

The outer layer is copper. This layer covers the frame. There are more than 300 sheets of copper. Each sheet is the width of two pennies. **Rivets** hold the sheets together.

The inside of the statue is filled with metal beams.

Chapter 3

Liberty Lighting the World

The Statue of Liberty reminds people of events from history. The statue holds a tablet. A date is written on it. It says "July 4, 1776." That is when the United States declared independence.

 **The date on the tablet is written in Roman numerals.**

The statue stands on broken chains. They are a symbol of slavery ending. That happened in 1865.

Many **immigrants** came to New York City by ship in the 1800s. They saw the Statue of Liberty when they arrived. When people see the statue today, they think of these immigrants.

Many groups have taken care of the Statue of Liberty. At first, the Lighthouse Board was in charge. Then the US Army looked after

 For many immigrants, the Statue of Liberty was a symbol of hope.

it. Finally, the government took control. US leaders wanted to protect the statue. So, they made it a national monument. Today, park rangers take care of the statue.

The Statue of Liberty is known around the world. In 1984, the United Nations made it a World Heritage Site. That means it is an important part of human history.

Many people worked together to build the Statue of Liberty. It was not easy. But they did it. The statue

Did You Know?

Emma Lazarus was a Jewish poet. She wrote a poem about the Statue of Liberty. The poem is on display inside the pedestal.

 Over the years, the statue has been repaired several times.

became a symbol of the human spirit. It is also a symbol of peace and friendship.

Chapter 4

Visiting the Statue

A visit to the Statue of Liberty starts with a **ferry** ride. Ferries leave from New York City and New Jersey. The ride takes 15 to 30 minutes. The ferry stops at Ellis Island and Liberty Island.

 **Ferries stop at Liberty Island many times each day.**

Ellis Island is where many immigrants arrived when they came to the United States. Today, the island has a museum. Here, visitors learn about immigrants. They can see many photos and old objects.

The Statue of Liberty is on Liberty Island. The island has several walking paths. Visitors can make

Did You Know?

More than 12 million immigrants entered the United States at Ellis Island.

On Liberty Island, visitors get excellent views of the statue.

their way around the statue. They
can also walk around the edge of
the island.

People also visit the Statue of Liberty Museum. It tells the story of the statue. The museum displays the original torch. Many people take pictures in front of it. A new torch was built in 1986.

People also visit the top of the pedestal. They can take an elevator or walk up the stairs. It is 10 stories high. From there, some people go inside the statue. They go all the way up to the crown. There is no elevator inside the statue. So, visitors must walk up 146 steps.

From the crown, visitors can see New York City. Many visitors also think about what the statue means to them. They think about peace, friendship, and freedom.

FOCUS ON
The Statue of Liberty

Write your answers on a separate piece of paper.

1. Write a sentence describing the symbols on the Statue of Liberty.

2. Would you go up to the Statue of Liberty's crown? Why or why not?

3. Who came up with the idea for the Statue of Liberty?
> **A.** Gustave Eiffel
> **B.** Édouard de Laboulaye
> **C.** Frédéric-Auguste Bartholdi

4. What makes the Statue of Liberty a symbol of friendship?
> **A.** It was a gift from France to the United States.
> **B.** It has a pedestal that is 10 stories high.
> **C.** It makes people think of immigrants.

5. What does **stable** mean in this book?

*Eiffel was a French engineer. He made sure the statue would be **stable**.*

    A. able to come up with new ideas
    B. unlikely to move or break
    C. from a different country

6. What does **displays** mean in this book?

*The museum **displays** the original torch. Many people take pictures in front of it.*

    A. shows something to visitors
    B. keeps something hidden away
    C. breaks something into pieces

Answer key on page 32.

Glossary

architect
Someone who designs structures and makes construction plans.

engineer
A person who designs buildings or structures.

ferry
A boat used to move people, vehicles, or goods from one place to another.

immigrants
People who move to a new country.

independent
Able to make decisions without being controlled by another government.

monument
A building or structure that is of historical interest or importance.

pedestal
The base that a statue is built on.

rivets
Bolts that hold pieces of metal together.

symbols
Things that stand for and remind people of other things or ideas.

To Learn More

BOOKS

Byrd, Robert. *Liberty Arrives!: How America's Grandest Statue Found Her Home.* New York: Dial Books for Young Readers, 2019.

Rajan, Rekha S. *Amazing Landmarks: Discover the Hidden Stories Behind 10 Iconic Structures!* New York: Scholastic, 2022.

Spanier, Kristine. *Statue of Liberty.* Minneapolis: Jump!, 2022.

NOTE TO EDUCATORS

Visit **www.focusreaders.com** to find lesson plans, activities, links, and other resources related to this title.

Index

Answer Key: 1. Answers will vary; 2. Answers will vary; 3. B; 4. A; 5. B; 6. A